ACROSS THE SILENCE

ACROSS

THE

SILENCE

Paintings

Sara Philpott

Haiku

Caroline Gourlay

HAIDUK PRESS
IN ASSOCIATION WITH
FIVE SEASONS PRESS

Published by
Haiduk Press
Hill House, Knighton
Powys LD7 1NA
and
Five Seasons Press
41 Green Street
Hereford HR1 2QH

ISBN 978-0-947960-69-8

Typeset in 18pt Ehrhardt at Five Seasons Press
and printed by Berforts Information Press

Foreword

I was brought up in South Shropshire and an untrammelled 1940s childhood of seemingly endless summers among its generous hills brought home to me a sense of where I belonged. Sara, raised in Surrey and subsequently studying art in London, came later in her life to the Welsh border country; she visited it in her twenties and, finding all the inspiration she needed for her art, has never left.

Our mutual love of the area has been an important ingredient in our friendship and one day while discussing the relative merits (and risks) of combining words and paintings into an art form, we started to play with the idea of making a book together — a book that would express, in haiku and paintings, our appreciation of a landscape we wanted to share with others for whom it might still be unexplored territory.

If it is not to become too diffuse, such an undertaking needs boundaries. When we had agreed on the basis for our project, we drew an invisible line defining a radius of about three miles, the compass point midway between Clun and Bishop's Castle, and set out to work within those limits. It seemed important that during this time we worked independently of each other and that, in order to experience fully the countryside — woods, hills, farms and hamlets — in its varying moods and seasons we would need a year. At the end of that time we agreed to meet, discuss and compare our responses to the chosen area and to discover how far what we had created individually reflected the same landscape.

When the twelve months were up we got together again to pool our experience and discovered some interesting differences and contrasts in our personal interpretations of, and approach to, the year's work. The next phase, therefore, was to set about combining what we had produced individually into a varied but coherent whole. For me this entailed discarding some of the haiku I had written during that time and replacing them with others inspired directly by one or other of Sara's paintings; I also included two haiku from an earlier collection. For her it meant leaving to one side some of the paintings that didn't resonate with what I had written.

Undoubtedly in all art forms the mood and state of mind of the artist will interact with, and colour the interpretation of the chosen subject. Some of Sara's paintings are disturbing and I am aware that the haiku of mine that seem to reflect this *angst* come from an awareness of the threat of climate change that hangs over all of us and the apparent inability, so far at least, of human beings to respond appropriately to its challenge. Things are already changing. It is impossible any longer to walk in the countryside and take for granted that it will continue in the timeless way it always has — to believe that Gaia, regardless of what we do to her, will always reassuringly be there for us, able to adapt to, and survive all we throw at her.

Nevertheless, awareness of this underlying unease has in no way detracted from the pleasure in what has been a hugely enjoyable collaborative experience for us both: the putting together of this book which, after passing through many stages, has finally settled into what you hold in your hands.

Caroline Gourlay

dawn meditation
a trout breaks the surface
of the hidden pool

light lifts the hills —
rising with the sun
a skylark's song

setting free
the sheep's wool from the wire —
a travelling wind

lambing over —
a pair of blackbirds
share a worm

a child
standing on his hands
walks on the sky

days of rain
drenched with catkins
the alder

spring returning . . .
the sound of a tractor drives
through an open door

looking for you —
overwhelmingly white
the lengthening road

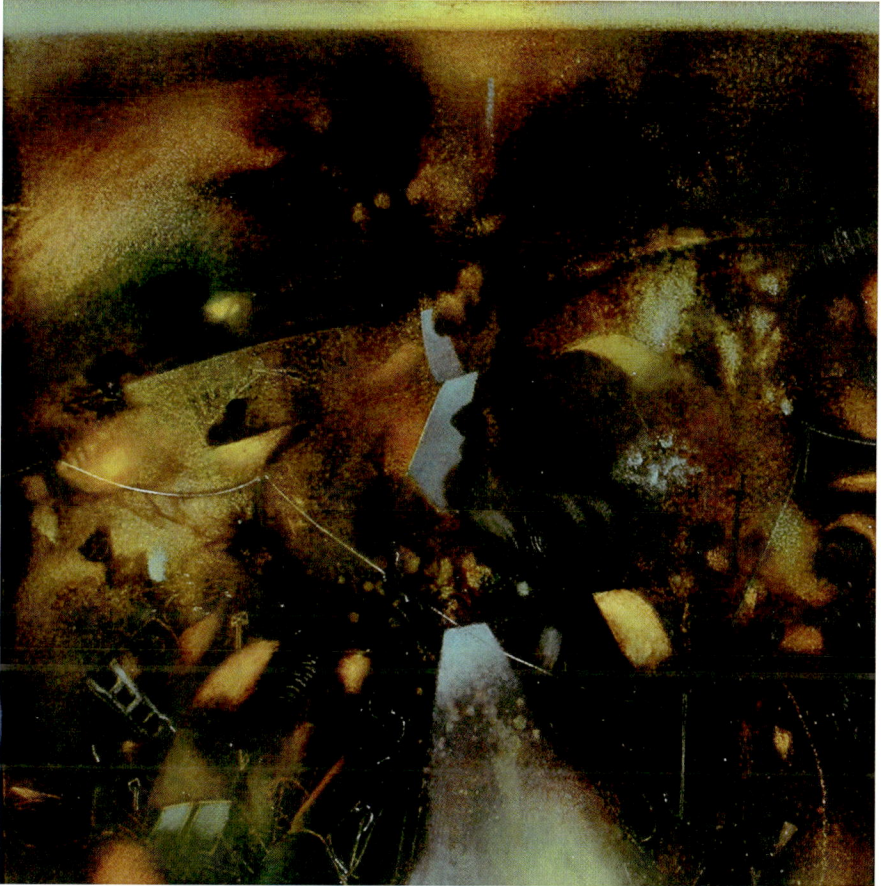

windows flung open
from Mainstone to Bryn Hill
the galloping woods

empty church —
a money-spider inches
down the pulpit

closing my eyes . . .
waterfall of silence
through the rafters

return journey
the child's coat still hanging
on the hedge

wind subsiding
shadows of a silver birch
steady the path

early morning mist
gathering in the lane
cow-parsley

dream
almost forgotten —
first spring walk

dark forest pool
a boy skims his flat stone
across the silence

cat washing herself—
such concentrated whiteness
of the long barn wall

'come home' you say . . .
silence settles on
a hawk moth's wing

back in the stream
the pike's brute ugliness
softens to gold

last light
slipping into the pool
a water vole

carrying it
around with me all day —
last night's quarrel

from behind tall pines
sun pushes a corn field
into the valley

farrier's van
the hammer heat of summer
blow by blow

South Shropshire . . .
a blue thread flowing free
I pull towards me

Cowpasture Farm
the setting sun leaves me
at the gate

path tailing off . . .
a red kite spreads its wings
into the rain

ageing too
I touch the old pine tree
— Spring

engine switched off —
leaning against an oak tree
afternoon sun

echo of wolves . . .
before voices and farmed land
these layered rocks

leaving behind
an abandoned campsite
the racing rain

storm receding . . .
a wet leaf expands
into sunlight

reflections fading
no one looking out now
to watch the trees

framed by the window
the sky
approaches winter

stopping the postman —
with each day fewer leaves
on the cherry tree

my pace slower —
beginning to notice
the days shorten

waiting
for the right moment to tell you —
leaves turning

long evening . . .
getting up from my chair
to light a candle

waking late
the sky empty
of swallows

wrong turning . . .
behind advancing trees
more trees

climate change . . .
hauling on his muscles
the squirrel leaps

failed harvest
a combine drives across the
glass blue sky

insomnia . . .
through the door in my head
another door

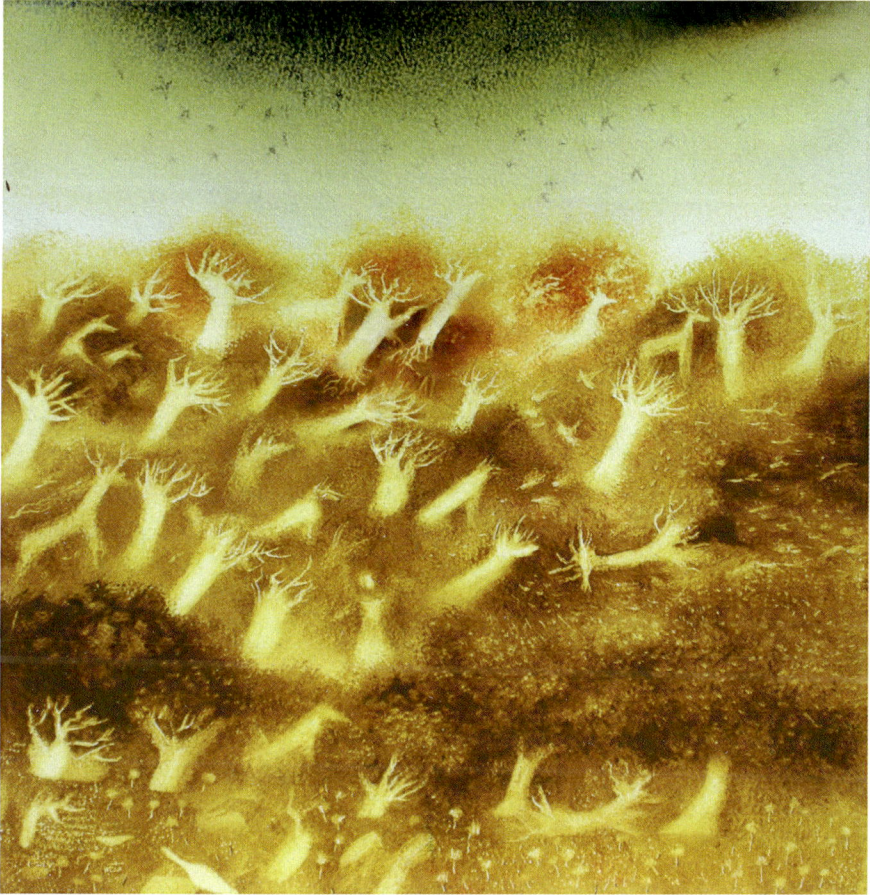

driving rain
passing through my sleep
a lapwing's cry

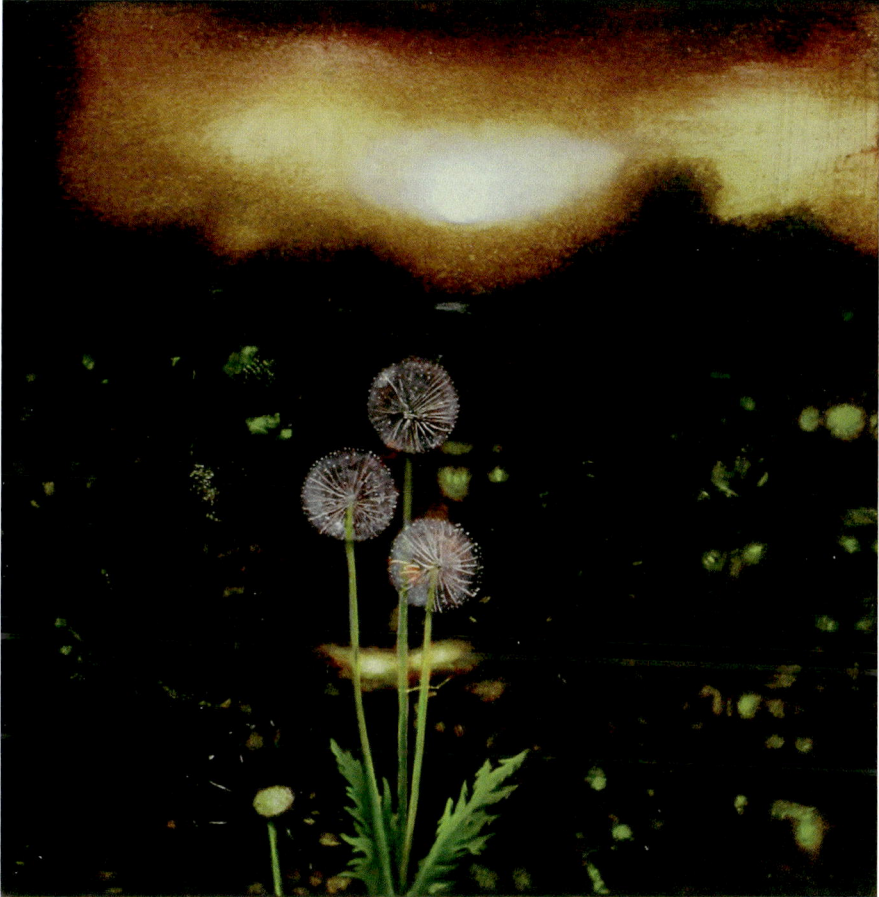

trying to open
this frozen landscape
the sun's blunt rays

a trap springs . . .
the rabbit's footprints
fill with snow

slowing to sludge . . .
river of birdsong
through the valley

wind turbine
almost at midnight
the clock's hands

reading it —
wanting to turn off
the full moon

melting ice floes
bluer and bluer
the scorched flower

Acknowledgements

Special thanks are due to the editors of the following publications in which some of these haiku first appeared or are due to appear: *Haiku Society of America Members Anthology 2010*, *Shamrock (Haiku Ireland)*, *Presence*, *Planet*, *Blithe Spirit* and *Muttering Thunder* (ebook anthology).